You are waiting for your king from the King,
but are you personally ready and whole?

This Journal Belongs To:

_____

Date:

_____

WAITING FOR YOUR KING

from the

King

Barbara Nelson Bennett

Lauderhill, FL

Learn more about the author at:
https://barbaranbennett.com

Cover design by Gabyriella Foster

Edited by Annette Purkiss, Allwrite Publishing

ISBN: 979-8-9918479-1-9

Library of Congress Control Number: 2024950729

Printed in the United States of America

Author's Note

A dear friend from prep school in Jamaica visited New York and met a man she believed was destined for me. She didn't call him a potential boyfriend; she confidently declared, "I have a husband for you." Intrigued yet skeptical, I questioned why she, eager for marriage herself, would introduce him to me.

Back in Florida, I hesitated but eventually agreed to a phone introduction. Aware of the challenges of a long-distance relationship, I candidly shared my desires and expectations with him, encouraging him to reflect on them. To my delight, he sought the same. Meeting each other's families was crucial to me, and the turning point came when he expressed, "I want you to meet my mom, and if she approves, I will marry you." This sincerity led me to delve into his background, and soon after, we began planning our wedding.

We were married within four months, and I can wholeheartedly say I would choose this man again. He exemplifies that faithfulness and genuine love are possible. I affectionately call him my "one burner man."

To all the single women reading this, I say remain open to the unexpected while you're waiting. Love often arrives in unforeseen ways. Trust in your journey, be clear about your desires, and embrace the possibilities that come your way. Your story is still unfolding, and it holds the promise of beautiful surprises.

Whether you are navigating the excitement or challenges of singleness, this journal aims to be a source of encouragement and strength as you await God's perfect plan for your life regarding a mate. I attempted to do it on my own, following my own path, believing that I could make things happen for myself. The truth is that in doing so, I wandered aimlessly, much like the children of Israel. God knows best.

While we may think we understand what we want for our lives, God knows what we truly need. When you begin to surrender your will and your life fully to God, that is when you will witness His hand at work in your life. You will reap the blessings. Just because you find yourself in a season that feels prolonged does not mean God has neglected you or has said no. It simply indicates that you are in a waiting season, and your waiting is not in vain.

As you journey through this journal, my prayer is that you embrace this season of waiting not with frustration, but with faith. The idea of a "one-burner man" is a metaphor, one that represents a man who chooses to love, commit, and nurture only one relationship: yours. He's not distracted by other "burners" on the stove. He's focused, intentional, and faithful.

However, before you meet that kind of man, you must become the kind of woman who is whole emotionally, spiritually, and mentally. This journal is not about waiting passively. It's about preparing actively. It's about turning inward to heal from past trauma, build genuine self-confidence, deepen your identity in Christ, and establish standards that are both godly and grounded.

This journal is founded on biblical principles and offers you a space to reflect, pray, and grow. Whether you are praying for your future spouse or embracing your current season of life, this book will help you remain grounded in the truth that the King is with you every step of the way. So, take a deep breath, grab a pen, and prepare to embark on this journey of faith, trust, and transformation. You are not alone, for God is at work, even in the waiting.

With grace and expectancy,

CONTENTS

ACKNOWLEDGMENTS

To my husband, Delroy Bennett—my rock. Thank you for being the man God has called you to be. You are truly my king from the King, and I am blessed to walk this journey with you.

To my sister, Audrey Nelson Campbell—thank you for always pushing me toward my greater purpose and standing by my side. Your support and encouragement mean the world to me. I couldn't ask for a better sister.

To my mother, Dorothy M. Nelson—your sacrifices and hard work have not gone unnoticed. Your labor has not been in vain, and you are deeply blessed. I love and honor you for all you've done and for the beautiful person you are.

To my son, Daner B. Hargrove—God has a plan for your life, one filled with hope, purpose, and promise. You are a blessing, a precious gift, and deeply loved. Never forget that.

To Bishop Rohan Diedrick, my mentor who baptized me and taught me how to have faith.

To Joan Quinland, my best friend and the person who witnessed to me, leading me to Christ.

And finally to Claudine Mighty for helping me proof read this book.

BEFORE WE BEGIN...

Welcome to "Waiting on Your King from the King," a journal designed to guide and encourage you during one of the most transformative seasons of your life. This journey is about much more than waiting for a relationship—it's about becoming the woman God has called you to beforehand. By focusing on your spiritual growth, self-discovery, and God's perfect plan, for your life this journal equips you with practical tools, biblical wisdom, and reflective exercises to help you embrace the fullness of life while preparing your heart for a future rooted in divine love.

Each chapter builds on the idea that waiting is not passive but purposeful. Here's a brief look at what you can expect as you work through this journal:

Defining Wholeness Through Faith

Discover the biblical foundations of wholeness and how it differs from the unrealistic pursuit of perfection. This chapter invites you to understand God's vision for your life, grounded in His love and grace.

Your Identity and How It Shapes Your Life

Explore who you are in Christ (Ephesians 1:11) and how your identity influences every aspect of your life. Reflect on your core values, confront fears and limiting beliefs, and develop emotional intelligence to navigate life with confidence and clarity.

Trusting God's Timing

Learn to trust in God's perfect plan and timing for your future. With biblical encouragement like Habakkuk 2:3, this chapter helps you release the pressure of societal timelines and embrace the peace that comes from surrendering to His will.

Strengthening Your Faith in Waiting

Deepen your trust in God by practicing surrender, leaning on prayer and devotion, and cultivating godly confidence and self-worth. This chapter encourages you to see waiting as a time to strengthen your relationship with Him before ever meeting him.

BEFORE WE BEGIN...

Becoming the Woman God Has Called You to Be
Find joy and contentment in your season of singleness (1 Corinthians 7:34) while practicing patience, humility, and kindness (Galatians 5:22-23). Embrace this time as an opportunity for personal and spiritual growth.

Fostering a Purposeful Life
Understand your God-given purpose (Jeremiah 29:11) and how to align your gifts and strengths with His plan. This chapter shows you how purpose can serve as preparation for future blessings.

Becoming Whole for Your King
Prepare your heart for future love by celebrating your wholeness and independence in Christ. This chapter reminds you that becoming the best version of yourself is the greatest gift you can bring to your future relationship.

Conclusion: Becoming Whole & Ready for Love
The journey to wholeness is one of self-discovery, spiritual growth, and unwavering faith. This closing chapter ties everything together, affirming that as you wait on God, He is preparing you for a love story that reflects His own commitment and grace.

Final Prayer
End your journey with a heartfelt prayer, seeking God's continued guidance and thanking Him for His love and perfect timing.

As you begin this journal, remember that waiting on your King is not about finding someone to complete you but about walking in the fullness of who God created you to be. Let this journey transform your heart, renew your faith, and draw you closer to God's divine purpose for your life.

DEFINING WHOLENESS THROUGH FAITH

Biblical Foundations of Wholeness

I remember telling my husband when we first met that I desired a man of God, someone who would lead me closer to God, not away from Him. He didn't hesitate. He didn't try to dissuade me from my desire. He agreed wholeheartedly, and that agreement was confirmation for me. When you make God's presence your standard, you won't be easily swayed by counterfeit versions of love.

Sometimes, we set lofty or even unreasonable standards for a partner, forgetting to measure ourselves against those same expectations. Do you seek a generous man while holding back your own resources? Do you want someone emotionally available while you avoid vulnerability? This journal will challenge you to examine not just what you want in a partner, but who you are becoming as a partner in Christ before ever fully knowing or even meeting your king from the King.

Yes, opposites may attract. We're often drawn to traits we admire but don't possess. Yet, at the core, your values must align. Differences in personality can add flavor, but unity in faith, family ideals, and vision provides the foundation.

As you wait on your King from the King, do so in faith, in purpose, and in wholeness. You are not waiting for completion. You are being refined in your completeness.

The Bible presents a consistent, profound message about the importance of wholeness — spiritual, emotional, and moral — before we step into roles where others may rely on us, such as a wife, mother, or leader. Scripture does not teach that we become whole through relationships, but that we are called to be whole in God before we can pour into others from a healthy, godly place.

Biblically, women are not waiting for a person or position to complete them. Rather, they are in a process of refinement so that they can enter relationships and lead others from a place of wholeness. This means their worth, stability, peace, and love are anchored in God, not in circumstances or titles.

Here are a few foundational principles and passages:

1. Wholeness Comes Through Christ

"You are complete in Him, who is the head of all principality and power."
— Colossians 2:10 (NKJV)

This verse clearly affirms that our completeness is found in Christ alone, not in a relationship, a title, or a role. Before a woman becomes a wife or mother, her identity and wholeness must be rooted in Him.

2. Love Your Neighbor as Yourself

"You shall love your neighbor as yourself." — Mark 12:31 (ESV)

This command assumes self-awareness and self-love rooted in God's love. A woman who hasn't learned to love herself in a healthy, God-centered way will struggle to love others fully, consistently or sincerely. Wholeness enables true interdependence.

3. Fruitfulness Flows from Abiding, Not Striving

"I am the vine; you are the branches. If you remain in me and I in you, you will bear much fruit; apart from me you can do nothing." — John 15:5 (NIV)

Roles like wife, mother or leader require spiritual fruit: patience, wisdom, grace. However, we can only bear that fruit if we are already abiding in the vine. Wholeness precedes fruitfulness.

4. God Builds from a Strong Foundation

"Everyone then who hears these words of mine and does them will be like a wise man who built his house on the rock." — Matthew 7:24 (ESV)

Jesus emphasizes that a life built on His words is stable and enduring. A whole woman builds her identity and emotional/spiritual life on His truth, so when she takes on roles with others depending on her, she does not crumble under the weight of pressure or people-pleasing.

5. Women Are Called to Be Whole, Not Waiting to Be Made Whole

"Let endurance have its full effect, so that you may be mature and complete, lacking nothing." — James 1:4 (CSB)

The refining process God uses — often in solitude or in seasons of waiting — is not about incompleteness, but about maturity. This verse makes clear: You are not waiting to be completed; you are being refined in your completeness.

REFLECT

In what ways have you sought completion through relationships, titles, or roles instead of anchoring your wholeness in Christ? What steps can you take to begin rooting you identity more deeply in Him?

_____

_____

_____

_____

_____

_____

_____

_____

_____

_____

_____

_____

_____

_____

_____

REFLECT

Ask yourself: Am I becoming the kind of woman I'm praying for in a partner: emotionally healed, spiritually grounded, and whole? If not, what areas of my life is God gently asking me to surrender for refinement?

_____

_____

_____

_____

_____

_____

_____

_____

_____

_____

_____

_____

_____

Differentiating Wholeness from Perfection

Wholeness is not the absence of flaws; it's the presence of growth, humility, and divine alignment. So often, we mistake being "ready for love" with being perfect, never making mistakes, never feeling triggered, never struggling. However, God's desire isn't for you to be flawless. It's for you to be faithful.

You have to identify those areas that you need to improve on because a lot of times, relationships don't work because you haven't worked on yourself. You may find yourself trying to get your mate to work on himself, but you yourself don't work on your own shortcomings. In Matt. 7:5, Jesus said, "First, cast out that beam from your own eye, and then you shall see clearly to cast out the splinter from your brother's eye." The Bible invites us to examine our own hearts, not someone else's.

Perfection tries to control others but wholeness lets God transform you and others. Many relationships unravel not because one person is "bad," but because both individuals are trying to fix each other or blame the other person rather than doing the inner work to which God calls us. True wholeness begins when you stop managing others' behavior and start humbling yourself before God, asking Him to reveal what needs healing in you.

Psalm 139:23–24 *"Search me, God, and know my heart; test me and know my anxious thoughts. See if there is any offensive way in me..."* (NIV)

Wholeness isn't about never falling; it's about trusting God to catch you.
Perfection says, "I must do it all right."
Wholeness says, "God is doing a work in me, and I trust His process."

Philippians 1:6 *"Being confident of this, that he who began a good work in you will carry it on to completion..."* (NIV)

Ultimately, you just have to deepen your faith in God and start trusting Him more rather than focus on whether you are perfect or even perfectly ready.

REFLECT

In what areas of your life have you been chasing perfection (e.g. physical, occupational, relational) instead of pursuing spiritual growth? How has this interfered with your spiritual growth?

_____

_____

_____

_____

_____

_____

_____

_____

_____

_____

_____

_____

_____

_____

Cultivating Godly Confidence & Self-Worth

Low self-esteem is often rooted in trauma and abuse. Wholeness is rooted in God-esteem. Low self-esteem often manifests as neediness, insecurity, or a tendency to define oneself through another person's affection. This creates pressure, not partnership. You have to work on your self-esteem before getting into a committed relationship. You can actually kill a relationship if your self-esteem is low. God wants to fill you with an unshakeable identity before you give your heart to another. That means your confidence must be in His love, not someone else's attention.

1 John 4:16 *"So we have come to know and to believe the love that God has for us."* (ESV)

When we bring unresolved wounds, unrealistic expectations, or past disappointments into new relationships, we sabotage what could be healthy with what hasn't yet healed. For me, I had deep trust issues. In all my previous relationships, the men had cheated or was already involved. So, I had no confidence in men or myself beyond superficial physical attributes. While I may have looked like a millionaire dollars, I had about $2 worth of self-esteem.

I definitely had trust issues when I first met Delroy, but he reassured me that he wasn't the type of man to cheat. But because of my own insecurities, I asked him to make our relationship status public on Facebook, and he did just that. That small action helped ease my fears and reassured me that he was serious about our connection. Honestly, if Delroy hadn't publicly acknowledged our relationship, I don't know if I would have felt secure, especially with me living in Fort Lauderdale and him in New York at the time.

Through our courtship, I realized how much I still needed to grow in my own confidence and worth. It wasn't just about trusting him; it was about trusting God and allowing Him to heal the parts of me that still felt unworthy, fearful or easily shaken. Godly confidence, what I call "God-esteem," is different from self-esteem. It's not built on how others have treated you or what they do or don't do to prove their love. It's built on who God is and who He says you are, considering the unwavering love He already gives.

REFLECT

Do you find yourself seeking reassurance from others to feel secure, or are you learning to rest in the confidence that comes from knowing who you are in Christ? Where might you still be relying on external validation?

_____

_____

_____

_____

_____

_____

_____

_____

_____

_____

_____

_____

_____

_____

REFLECT

What past experiences or insecurities have shaped the way you see yourself in relationships and how can you invite God to heal and redefine your worth through His truth?

_____

_____

_____

_____

_____

_____

_____

_____

_____

_____

_____

_____

_____

_____

Resting in Divine Love

God's Word teaches us what love truly looks like—how it's patient, kind, not self-seeking or boastful. It's right there in Scripture, and yet, for a long time, I didn't know how to apply those truths to my own life. I didn't know how to rest in God's love or see myself the way He sees me.

I began using affirmations to speak life over myself. I'd say, "I'm wonderful. I'm beautiful. I'm a princess deserving of God's best. I am bold and confident." I had to start believing those words because before that, I was a woman deeply wounded, battered emotionally, and unsure of my worth. Looking back, I believe that's why I kept attracting the wrong men.

For years, I was drawn to men like my ex. I knew he was juggling multiple women, yet I waited by the phone, hoping he'd call and decide that I was the one for him. I stayed in that cycle for 14 years on and off. If I had known my worth, if I had truly loved and valued myself, I would have never settled for being an option instead of a priority.

The truth is, I spent my youth waiting on a man to become what only God could shape. It wasn't until I fully surrendered—until I allowed God to take control of my life—that everything began to change. I started letting go of the things I had clung to out of fear, pride or vanity. And in doing so, I found something far greater: peace. Not from a man, but from God. Because He knows what's best for you, even when you can't see it yet.

Romans 8:38–39 *"For I am convinced that neither death nor life, neither angels nor demons, neither the present nor the future, nor any powers... will be able to separate us from the love of God that is in Christ Jesus our Lord."* (NIV)

Resting in His love means no longer striving, chasing, or settling. It means allowing His love to fill the empty places so you don't go searching for it in someone else's brokenness. God's love is constant, unshakable, and complete. When you rest in His love, you stop chasing incomplete versions of it in others.

REFLECT

Are there areas in your life where you've been waiting on someone to give you the love, attention, or value that only God can provide? How has that shaped your self-worth?

_____

_____

_____

_____

_____

_____

_____

_____

_____

_____

_____

_____

_____

_____

_____

REFLECT

What fears or past hurts are you still holding onto that may be keeping you from fully surrendering to God's love? What would it look like to let them go?

_____

_____

_____

_____

_____

_____

_____

_____

_____

_____

_____

_____

_____

_____

_____

REFLECT

Can you identify a time when you settled for less than you deserved because you didn't see yourself the way God sees you? What truth from God's Word can you begin to declare over yourself instead?

_____

_____

_____

_____

_____

_____

_____

_____

_____

_____

_____

_____

_____

Work Out Your Faith

Walking in Wholeness

Step 1: **Ground Yourself in Scripture**

Read one of the following scriptures each day or week. Ask God to show you what it reveals about wholeness in Him.

- Colossians 2:10 – "You are complete in Him..."
- Romans 8:38–39 – Nothing can separate you from God's love.
- Philippians 1:6 – God is completing a good work in you.
- Psalm 139:23–24 – Invite God to search and reveal your heart.

📖 Write down one truth that stands out to you and how it applies to your life today.

Step 2: **Speak Life Over Yourself**

Say and write these affirmations daily for the next 7 days. Then, write your own.

🗣 Say aloud:

- **I am whole in Christ.**
- **I am worthy of love and respect.**
- **I release the past and receive God's healing.**
- **I trust God's timing and plan for my life.**

Step 3: **Rest in His Love**

Find 10 minutes of quiet time. No phone. No distractions.

🙏 In silence or prayer, ask:

Lord, where am I still striving? Show me how to rest in Your love instead.

✒️ Write what comes to your heart. It may be a word, an image, a memory, or a scripture.

AFFIRMATION
of
Faith

I am wonderfully and intentionally made. Every part of me is known by God, down to the very number of my hair strands. He was intricately involved in my creation, and nothing about me is a mistake. I am His masterpiece.

Now, Write Your Own...

_____

_____

_____

_____

_____

_____

EMBRACING SELF-AWARENESS

Who You Are in Christ

As women of God, understanding your identity in Christ is foundational. So often, the world tries to define you by your outward appearance, your relationship status, your past, or even your failures. But God sees you through the lens of grace, love, and purpose.

In this section, we will dive deep into what it means to be a daughter of the King —chosen, loved, and set apart. This is not about superficial affirmations but embracing the raw, unchanging truth of who you are in Christ. Temporary circumstances do not define you but by the eternal love of your Creator.

Ephesians 1:4-5 NLT

Even before He made the world, God loved us and chose us in Christ to be holy and without fault. God decided in advance tinto His own family by bringing us to Himself through Jesus Christ. This is what He wanted to do, and it gave Him great pleasure.

You were chosen by God before you even took your first breath. His decision to adopt you into His family wasn't an afterthought—it was His joy and pleasure. Think about that. The Creator of the universe handpicked you to be His daughter. There's no need to seek validation or worth from anyone else because you are already loved beyond measure.

Psalm 139:13-16 NLT

For you created my inmost being; you knit me together in my mother's womb. I praise you because I am fearfully and wonderfully made; your works are wonderful, I know that full well. My frame was not hidden from you when I was made in the secret place, when I was woven together in the depths of the earth. Your eyes saw my unformed body; all the days ordained for me were written in your book before one of them came to be.

REFLECT

How has not knowing your identity in Christ affected your relationships and decisions in the past? Look back at choices you've made when you didn't know your true worth. How did a lack of identity impact those choices? What can you learn from those moments?

REFLECT

What patterns of self-sabotage do you notice in your life? Are there areas where you intentionally or unintentionally destroy your progress or relationships because you feel unworthy? Explore how this behavior is connected to your identity and how God might be inviting you to break free from it.

Examining Your Core Values

When I think back to meeting Delroy, I realize how important it was for me to be clear on my values—before I got too emotionally invested. From the beginning, I knew I needed a man who shared my faith. I asked him straight up if he was a Christian. He told me he wasn't, but that he knew about God because he grew up going to church with his family. That wasn't enough for me. I told him, "If you really want to date me, you need to know who God is."

To my surprise, he started going to church on his own. He found a Pentecostal church in New Jersey because I had shared that's the kind of church I wanted to attend. It mattered deeply to me that I wouldn't have to drag someone to worship on Sunday mornings. I needed a man who was seeking God for himself.

Beyond faith, I also wanted to know how he felt about me having a son. When he shared that he also had a child and co-parented with his ex-wife, that opened the door to a deeper conversation. I asked what caused his previous relationship to end. He answered, but I could sense some deeper pain there, like maybe his ex-wife had made him feel small or less than.

For the first time in my life, I also asked about money. I wanted to know about his spending habits and income. I had never been bold enough to ask those questions before, but since we were talking long distance, I felt like I had nothing to lose. Honestly, I didn't want to waste time, so from day one, I told him that if he wasn't thinking about marriage, he shouldn't even try to date me.

All of this taught me how important it is to examine your core values and not be afraid to express them. The Bible says in Amos 3:3, "Can two walk together, unless they are agreed?" If we're not aligned in the areas that matter most, we're building on shaky ground. If you desire a Christ-centered relationship, take time now to reflect on your own values. Don't wait until your heart is entangled to begin asking what really matters to you.

To uncover or clarify your core values, ask yourself questions like:

- What matters most to me in life and relationships?
- What behaviors or traits are deal-breakers?
- What do I need in order to feel emotionally and spiritually safe?

You can also look at what worked and what didn't in your past relationships. What values did you compromise? What did you learn about yourself? Don't just focus on what they did; look at your responses and patterns too.

REFLECT

What are three non-negotiable values you must share with a future partner? Are you willing to speak up early about these values, even if it means the relationship might not continue? If not, why?

_____

_____

_____

_____

_____

_____

_____

_____

_____

_____

_____

_____

_____

_____

REFLECT

How are your current decisions in dating, friendship or faith reflecting the values you say are important? How do your values align with biblical principles? (Use Galatians 5:22-23 and 1 Corinthians 13 to guide your answers.)

_____

_____

_____

_____

_____

_____

_____

_____

_____

_____

_____

_____

_____

_____

_____

Facing Fears and Limiting Beliefs

Too often, we fall for the lies the world tells us about our worth and identity through social media, family dynamics, cultural pressures, and even our past relationships. As a result, you may falsely believe:

- "I'm not beautiful enough."
- "I'm too flawed."
- "Women like me don't get opportunities like that."
- "I'm not worthy of a good man or a Godly man because…"

These lies can take root in your heart, causing you to question your value. But let's be real—these thoughts are not from God. The enemy wants you to live in insecurity and fear, but God has called you to live in the freedom of His truth.

The devil is our enemy, and he is called the "father of lies" for a reason. Deception is at the core of his nature. He twists the truth, distorts reality, and feeds us lies to pull us away from God's purpose for our lives. His goal is to prevent the people of God from prospering. He knows his fate—eternal separation from God in Hell—and in his misery, he desires to drag others down with him. He wants to ensure that he does not suffer alone. However, God is the complete opposite. It is impossible for Him to lie. Lying contradicts His very nature because God is truth. If He were to lie, He would no longer be true to who He is, and that would make Him no longer God. The Bible affirms again and again that God is unchanging, trustworthy, and faithful. Hebrews 13:8 reminds us, "Jesus Christ the same yesterday, and today, and forever."

More than that, God consistently affirms our identity in Him throughout Scripture. He created us in His image, perfectly designed by the hands of our Creator. Who are we to question His design? In God's eyes, you are beautifully and wonderfully made, and He knows you better than anyone ever could—even down to the number of hairs on your head (Luke 12:7).

Fear and limiting beliefs often disguise themselves as facts. But many of them were formed by past pain, negative words spoken by others, or doctrines rooted in spiritual doubt, not truth. To become the woman God has called you to be, you must learn to **recognize**, **reject**, and **replace** these lies with God's truth.

John 8:32 "Then you will know the truth, and the truth will set you free." (NIV)

Remember, God cannot lie!

If God has spoken something over your life—whether about your identity, your purpose, or your worth—it doesn't matter who tries to contradict it. It doesn't matter if your mother, father, best friend, coworker, or even the devil himself disagrees. What God has said **is true**. His word is unshakable because **He cannot lie**. If He has declared it, it is so. We need to challenge and pull down these thoughts and lies of the enemy when they come, holding on to what God says. Don't wait to feel confident. Act in faith. Every small step you take in spite of fear, weakens that lie's power over you.

Numbers 23:19

God is not a man, so He does not lie. He is not human, so he does not change his mind. Has He ever spoken and failed to act? Has he ever promised and not carried it through?

Hebrews 6:18

So God has given both his promise and his oath. These two things are unchangeable because it is impossible for God to lie. Therefore, we who have fled to him for refuge can have great confidence as we hold to the hope that lies before us.

REFLECT

How do you currently view your body in relation to your spiritual walk with God? Are there areas where you struggle to honor your body as a temple of the Holy Spirit? How has this affected you personally (e.g. health, self-worth) and your past relationships?

_____

_____

_____

_____

_____

_____

_____

_____

_____

_____

_____

_____

_____

REFLECT

What steps can you take to improve your emotional, spiritual, and physical well-being in preparation for a healthy, intimate relationship? In what ways have past experiences (emotional or physical) affected your ability to trust others? How can surrendering these struggles to God help restore your heart for future intimacy?

_____

_____

_____

_____

_____

_____

_____

_____

_____

_____

_____

_____

_____

Understanding Your Emotions and Emotional Intelligence

Emotional intelligence isn't just about how we manage our feelings—it's also about how well we understand others. One of the greatest signs of emotional maturity is the ability to listen with both the head and the heart.

I'll be honest, I had to learn how to listen. I was never naturally good at it. I'm a talker. And while someone else is speaking, I'm already thinking about what I'm going to say next. But over time, I realized that was hurting my relationships. I wasn't listening to understand; I was listening to respond. That's not communication. That's control.

Listening became one of my biggest lessons, especially in marriage. I learned that sometimes we're both saying the same thing—but we're not hearing each other because we're too busy defending instead of processing. That lack of emotional intelligence can turn small misunderstandings into unnecessary arguments.

📖 What Proverbs says about listening:
"The way of fools seems right to them, but the wise listen to advice."
— Proverbs 12:15 (NIV)
"A fool takes no pleasure in understanding, but only in expressing his opinion."
— Proverbs 18:2 (ESV)
"Even fools are thought wise if they keep silent, and discerning if they hold their tongues."
— Proverbs 17:28 (NIV)

These verses hit home for me. Before marriage, I thought I knew everything. I didn't seek wise counsel. I didn't slow down to listen not just to others, but to God. Like Proverbs says, I acted like a fool in those moments, but healing begins with humility.

Emotional intelligence in relationships includes:
- Listening without interrupting
- Pausing before responding
- Asking questions instead of making assumptions
- Recognizing emotional triggers
- Validating what the other person is feeling, even if you don't agree

Challenge:
Pick one conversation this week where you will intentionally listen without interrupting. Write down how it felt and what you learned.

Emotional Intelligence (EQ) is the God-given ability to understand, manage, and express your own emotions in healthy, constructive ways, while also being able to recognize, empathize with, and respond appropriately to the emotions of others. These are biblical principles that reflect one's EQ:

- **Self-Awareness & Self-Control**

In Scripture, this concept is closely related to wisdom, self-control, discernment, compassion, and love, all of which are traits the Bible repeatedly urges us to develop. Being emotionally intelligent means being aware of your feelings and how they influence your words, reactions, and decisions. The Bible calls this self-control, a fruit of the Spirit (Galatians 5:22–23).

- **Empathy & Compassion**

Recognizing and responding to the emotions of others with genuine care is a reflection of Christ's love. Emotional intelligence teaches us to listen, validate, and comfort others, just as Jesus did. In this regard, Romans 12:15 states, "Rejoice with those who rejoice; mourn with those who mourn."

- **Wisdom in Interactions**

The Bible advises that "every person be quick to hear, slow to speak, slow to anger" (James 1:19, ESV). EQ is about responding with intention, not reacting in emotion. This verse beautifully describes emotional maturity as being measured, thoughtful, and willing to listen.

- **Discernment & Emotional Boundaries**

Having emotional intelligence includes knowing when and how to protect your heart, set boundaries, and respond with discernment rather than impulsivity or fear. The Bible warns us to guard our heart because all our ideals flows from it (Prov. 4:23)

As you wait on your king, God is refining your character. Emotional intelligence is not just for dating or marriage, it's essential for friendships, leadership, ministry, and spiritual maturity. Developing emotional intelligence is one of the ways you prepare your heart to love and be loved in a Christlike way.

REFLECT

Ask yourself: Do I listen to understand or just to respond? When someone speaks to me, do I pause to process or prepare a rebuttal? Who do I need to listen to more intentionally, including God, a friend, a parent, or even myself?

_____

_____

_____

_____

_____

_____

_____

_____

_____

_____

_____

_____

_____

_____

REFLECT

Am you regularly practicing empathy and self-control in my relationships, or do you struggle to recognize and manage your emotions when your hurt, misunderstood or challenged?

_____

_____

_____

_____

_____

_____

_____

_____

_____

_____

_____

_____

_____

_____

_____

Work Out Your Faith

Embracing Myself

.Step 1: Identify the Falsehoods

✒ In your journal, write down the lies and limiting beliefs that you've believed about yourself. Be honest.

Example: "I'm not good enough to deserve a godly man," or "I'm too damaged by my past to be truly loved."

Step 2: Embrace the Truth

✒ Now, write down the truth from God's Word that replaces that lie and limiting beliefs.

Example: Lie: "I'm not good enough."

Truth: "I am fearfully and wonderfully made" (Psalm 139:14).

Example: Lie: "I'll never find true love."

Truth: "No good thing does He withhold from those who walk uprightly" (Psalm 84:11).

Step 3: Make the Declaration

🙏 Every morning for the next week, look at these truths, say them aloud, and declare them over yourself in prayer. This isn't just positive thinking; it's spiritual warfare, replacing the enemy's lies with God's truth.

Step 4: Write the Vision

✒ Write a **personal mission statement** for your life that outlines your core values and the person you want to become. Base it on biblical principles and God's calling for your life.

Reflection: After completing your mission statement, ask yourself, *"How is my life currently aligning with this mission? What steps can I take to live more intentionally according to this vision?"*

AFFIRMATION
of
Faith

I am not ruled by fear, doubt, or insecurity. God has not given me a spirit of fear, but of power, love, and a sound mind. I am being transformed by the renewing of my mind, and every lie that once limited me is being replaced with God's truth. I walk in courage, clarity, and confidence because He is with me.

Now, Write Your Own...

_____

_____

_____

_____

_____

_____

TRUSTING GOD'S TIMING

Trusting in God's Plan for Your Future

Waiting can feel agonizing, especially when you desire something good. Whether it's waiting for a godly relationship, a career breakthrough, or healing in a certain area of your life, waiting often feels like wandering through a desert. You may find yourself questioning if God has forgotten you or if He's withholding His blessings because you've done something wrong. But the truth is, waiting is often a time of preparation.

Waiting is not punishment. It's refinement. In these seasons, God is shaping you, molding you, and strengthening you for what lies ahead. To rush this process is to forfeit the beauty of what He is trying to do in your life. You cannot microwave spiritual maturity. It takes time, discipline, and patience.

Yet, in the heat of the waiting season, many fail to trust God's plan and settle for what's convenient rather than what's God-ordained. Settling can take on many forms: entering into a relationship with someone who isn't aligned with your faith, choosing a path because it seems easier, or compromising on the standards you once held dear because you're tired of waiting.

Here's the hard truth: Settling is the slow death of your destiny. Abraham and Sarah (Genesis 16-21): One of the most powerful examples of waiting (and the consequences of settling) is the story of Abraham and Sarah. God promised them a son, but after years of waiting, Sarah became impatient. She convinced Abraham to have a child with her maidservant, Hagar. Ishmael was born from this impatience, but it led to deep pain, jealousy, and division within their family.

God had not forgotten His promise. Even though Sarah was past childbearing age, God still gave them Isaac, the son He had promised all along. Settling for Ishmael may have seemed like a shortcut, but it caused unnecessary pain and hardship. Isaac, the child of promise, came in God's perfect timing, not theirs.

Just like Abraham and Sarah's choice with Hagar, settling often brings about unintended consequences. These consequences can affect not only you but also the people around you for generations. What seems like a small compromise can spiral into many years of hardship or confusion. In His mercy, God provided that Ishmael would be the father of "twelve princes" and a "great nation."

REFLECT

What voices are influencing your decision-making? Identify the people, culture, or situations that are pressuring you to settle or question God's timing. How can you silence those voices and refocus on God's truth?

_____

_____

_____

_____

_____

_____

_____

_____

_____

_____

_____

_____

_____

_____

_____

REFLECT

In what ways have you been trying to control the outcome of your future relationships instead of trusting God's timing and His plan for you? What fears or insecurities are driving your need to control?

_____

_____

_____

_____

_____

_____

_____

_____

_____

_____

_____

_____

_____

Dangers of Settling

Settling rather than waiting on God to direct your steps in finding a mate can lead to deep emotional, spiritual, and relational consequences. While the desire for companionship is natural and God-given, stepping ahead of His timing and choosing someone based on pressure, loneliness or fear, can hinder both your growth and peace. Here are some key dangers of settling:

1. Emotional Drain and Disappointment
Settling often means accepting less than what aligns with your values, needs or God-given vision for your life. Over time, this can lead to chronic dissatisfaction, resentment, and heartbreak.

"Hope deferred makes the heart sick..." – Prov. 13:12

When your soul knows you're settling, it struggles to rest.

2. Missing God's Best
When you settle, you may bypass the one God was preparing for you or miss a deeper work He was doing in you during your waiting season. God's best often requires trust, patience, and surrender. Settling can cut the process short.

"The Lord is good to those who wait for Him, to the soul who seeks Him." – Lam. 3:25

God's best often requires trust, patience, and surrender. Settling can cut the process short.

3. Unequally Yoked Partnerships
Choosing a mate who does not share your faith, purpose, or values can pull you out of alignment with God's will and lead to spiritual conflict.

"Do not be unequally yoked with unbelievers." – 2 Cor. 6:14

Settling for companionship at the cost of spiritual unity can slowly erode your convictions.

4. Compromising Your Calling

When you settle, you may align with someone who cannot support, share, or even understand your God-given purpose. This can delay or derail your growth.

"Many are the plans in a person's heart, but it is the Lord's purpose that prevails." – Prov. 19:21

A misaligned partnership can become a weight instead of a blessing.

5. Emotional Codependency or Identity Loss

Settling out of fear or insecurity can lead to relying on a person to fill what only God was meant to. This can breed codependency and blur your sense of self-worth.

"You are complete in Him..." – Col. 2:10

God never intended for a partner to complete you, only to complement you.

Settling trades short-term relief for long-term struggle. Waiting on God isn't passive; it's preparatory. It's a sacred season where He refines you, deepens your trust, and aligns your heart with His. Every time you settle, you train your heart to doubt God's goodness and faithfulness.

Furthermore, settling for less than what God has intended is a dangerous trap. It's a decision made out of impatience, fear, or desperation. The danger isn't just about "missing out" on something better. It's about living in disobedience to God's will. When you settle, you are essentially saying, "God, I don't trust Your timing."

REFLECT

Have you ever pursued or put up with someone you thought was from God, only to realize later that it wasn't? How did that experience shape your understanding of waiting for God's best? How did you feel in the aftermath? What lessons did you learn?

_____

_____

_____

_____

_____

_____

_____

_____

_____

_____

_____

_____

_____

_____

REFLECT

Think about how settling might affect your spiritual growth, emotional well-being, and relationship with God. What would you be giving up if you chose to settle instead of waiting for God's best? What would be the cost?

_____

_____

_____

_____

_____

_____

_____

_____

_____

_____

_____

_____

_____

_____

Patience in God's Promises

I had always believed God had a mate for me, and I truly felt I found him when I met my son's father. I just knew we he would chose me and we would have a loving, lasting marriage and family. Although that's what I wanted very badly at the time, I thank God that He never allowed him to marry me because that would have been a disaster. God knew better and protected me. Determined to operate in my timing and will, my challenge was being patient. Like many others, I had to learn to trust Him with my heart.

David was anointed king as a young man, but he didn't step into that role immediately (1 Samuel 16-2 Samuel 5). He spent years fleeing from King Saul, hiding in caves, and wondering when God's promise would be fulfilled. David had several opportunities to kill Saul and seize the throne, but he refused. He would not settle for the throne until God's timing made it clear.

David's story shows us that even though God may give us a glimpse of His plan, we must be patient for His timing. If David had taken matters into his own hands, he could have forfeited God's greater plan for him as Israel's king.

When you choose to wait on God's timing, you are actively choosing faith over fear. Waiting is not passive; it's a posture of trust. You're saying, "God, I trust You more than I trust my own desires. I believe You have something far better for me than I could create on my own."

And here's the thing: God's timing is perfect. He knows what He's doing. You may feel like you've been waiting forever, but there's purpose in the waiting. Maybe He's refining your character, or maybe He's orchestrating circumstances that you cannot yet see. Whatever it is, trust that He's working all things together for your good.

Proverbs 3:5-6 *"Trust in the Lord with all your heart, and lean not on your own understanding; in all your ways acknowledge Him, and He shall direct your paths."*

Waiting for God's promises, especially in the area of love, can feel like a test of your very soul. But patience isn't passive, and it's not punishment. It's preparation and development.

Here's how you can develop godly patience while trusting Him for a mate:

1. Remember That God is Not Slow. He is Strategic

"For the vision is yet for an appointed time... though it tarry, wait for it; because it will surely come, it will not delay."
— Habakkuk 2:3 (KJV)

God isn't stalling. He's aligning. There may be things in your heart, your future spouse's life, or your circumstances that He is still working on. Trust that delay is not denial. It's divine timing.

2. Focus on Becoming, Not Just Receiving

While waiting, God often focuses not on what you'll get, but who you're becoming.

"Let patience have her perfect work, that ye may be perfect and entire, wanting nothing."
— James 1:4 (KJV)

Patience matures us. Use this season to grow in faith, purpose, emotional intelligence, and self-love. A healthy marriage is built between two whole people, not two halves looking for completion.

3. Fill the Waiting with Purpose

"Delight yourself in the Lord, and He will give you the desires of your heart."
— Psalm 37:4 (NIV)

Don't make marriage your mission, make delighting in God your mission. When your joy is rooted in Him, you become anchored, not anxious.

4. Guard Against Comparison & Cultural Pressure

Social media and society often make it seem like everyone else is "ahead." However, your life is not on their timeline.

"Do not conform to the pattern of this world, but be transformed by the renewing of your mind."
— Romans 12:2 (NIV)

Release the pressure of other people's pace and trust that your story is unfolding exactly as it should.

PRAYER WALL

As I wait for the godly relationship, You are preparing me. I ask for wisdom. I don't want to be led by emotions or external pressures. Help me to discern the people who come into my life. Give me the wisdom to recognize whether they align with the vision You have for my life and the standards You've set for me. Guard my heart from settling for a relationship that is not rooted in You. Let me be guided by Your Spirit, not my own desires. Protect me from any relationship that would lead me away from You, and give me the patience to wait for a man after Your heart. Amen.

I pray for Your peace to settle deep in my soul as I wait. There are moments when anxiety tries to take over, when I feel like time is slipping away or that I'm missing out. But I know that You hold time in Your hands, and You are never late. You are always on time. Fill my heart with the peace that surpasses all understanding. Help me rest in the knowledge that You are in control, and that Your plans for me are good. Let me embrace this season with peace and contentment, trusting that in Your time, everything will come to pass. I place my hope and faith in You alone. Amen.

REFLECT

How would you feel if God asked you to wait longer than you expected?
Be honest. How does the thought of extended waiting make you feel: Angry?
Sad? Anxious? What scriptures can you meditate on to strengthen your
endurance in this season?

_____

_____

_____

_____

_____

_____

_____

_____

_____

_____

_____

_____

_____

REFLECT

Are you growing spiritually and emotionally in this season or simply waiting for someone else to arrive and fill a void? What do you have to do in order to gain greater trust and faith in God's divine love and truth for your life?

_____

_____

_____

_____

_____

_____

_____

_____

_____

_____

_____

_____

_____

_____

_____

Serving While Waiting

The Bible offers us examples of women who trusted in God's timing, prepared themselves, and were blessed with godly spouses. Let's take a deeper look at these stories and see what we can learn from their faith and patience.

Ruth's story is one of the most well-known examples of a woman waiting on God's timing. After her husband's death, Ruth remained loyal to her mother-in-law, Naomi, and returned with her to Bethlehem. Ruth didn't sit idly in her waiting. She worked hard to provide for Naomi and herself, gleaning in the fields where she eventually met Boaz. He was not only a man of great character but also God's provision for Ruth because of her loyalty and faithfulness.

Key Lessons from Ruth's Story:
- Ruth's heart was focused on serving others, being a blessing, rather than seeking a spouse.
- She trusted God with her future and remained faithful in her responsibilities.
- God rewarded her loyalty with a husband who deeply respected and cherished her.

Esther was another woman who waited on God and allowed Him to prepare her for a significant purpose. She didn't rush into her position as queen but instead spent time in preparation. Esther fasted and prayed before approaching King Xerxes, trusting God's timing and seeking His favor for her people.

Key Lessons from Esther's Story:
- Esther used her time of preparation wisely, drawing close to God in fasting and prayer.
- She did not act impulsively but waited for the right time to fulfill her purpose.
- Her faith and patience saved her people and secured her position as queen.

REFLECT

What can you do to serve a greater mission or calling that aligns with God's leading and Word? This could be an opportunity to serve in your home, school, work and/or community here or abroad.

_____

_____

_____

_____

_____

_____

_____

_____

_____

_____

_____

_____

_____

_____

Work Out Your Faith

Trusting One Day at a Time

Step 1: Release the Clock

"For the vision is yet for an appointed time... though it tarry, wait for it." – Habakkuk 2:3

On a blank page, write down every timeline or expectation you've had for love, marriage, or your future.

Then, symbolically cross them out and write:
"God's timing > My timeline."

Step 2: Meditate on His Plan

"'For I know the plans I have for you,' declares the Lord..." – Jeremiah 29:11

Read this verse slowly three times.

In your journal, write what you believe God might be preparing you for—even if you can't see it yet.

Step 3: Serve While You Wait

Ruth served Naomi faithfully, and God honored her in due season.

Ask yourself: How can I serve someone else [this week] joyfully and without expecting anything in return?

List one simple act of service you can do (a call, a gift, a prayer, a meal). Then do it.

Work Out Your Faith

Trusting One Day at a Time

Step 4: Recognize the Danger of Settling

🚩 List 3 non-negotiable qualities you know are essential in a God-centered partner.

Then ask: Am I ever tempted to compromise these just to feel chosen?

🎯 Circle the one you're most likely to waver on and pray for strength to stand firm.

Step 5: Declare Your Trust

Write or say aloud this short affirmation each day this week:

"God, I trust You. I release my timelines, my fears, and my desire to control the outcome. I believe that what You have for me is worth the wait."

Activity: Write a letter to your future self, describing how you want to feel when God's promises for your life have come to pass. Include a declaration that you will not settle for less than what God has ordained for you.

Reflection: Seal the letter and set a reminder to open it in a year, or when you feel tempted to compromise.

AFFIRMATION
of
Faith

I trust that God's timing is perfect. There is a season for everything, and what He has promised will come to pass at the appointed time. I will not rush ahead or lean on my own understanding. Instead, I surrender my timeline to Him, knowing that He is ordering my steps and working all things out for my good.

Now, Write Your Own...

_____

_____

_____

_____

_____

_____

BECOMING THE WOMAN GOD HAS CALLED YOU TO BE

Preparing Your Heart for Future Love

As you wait for the man God has destined for you, it's crucial to remember that this season is not just about waiting; it's about becoming who God wants you to be. God calls us not only to hope for our future partners but also to prepare ourselves to be the women He has created us to be. This journey of self-discovery and spiritual growth is foundational to attracting the right partner and fulfilling God's purpose for your life.

The first step in preparing to meet your future spouse is focusing on your relationship with God and becoming the woman He's called you to be. If you are not aligned with God's purpose and pursuing His will, you will miss the bigger picture—His plan for your life. **Proverbs 31:30** reminds us that "Charm is deceptive, and beauty is fleeting; but a woman who fears the Lord is to be praised." God calls you to be more than outwardly beautiful—He calls you to cultivate a heart that is full of wisdom, grace, and godliness.

Your purpose as a daughter of God is not just to wait for marriage but to walk in His calling for you. He has a plan specifically for you, and in the waiting season, He wants to mold and shape you into the woman He created you to be. Ephesians 2:10 says, "For we are His workmanship, created in Christ Jesus for good works, which God prepared beforehand, that we should walk in them."

When someone truly cares about you, they don't just say it, they show it through protection, honesty, and integrity. They don't lie, cheat, or manipulate. My husband is that kind of man. From my health to our finances, he consistently demonstrates that he values not only me, but also our union. He honors my heart.

However, before I could receive that kind of love, I had to care for my own heart first. I had to treat myself with the same level of respect I desired from someone else. That meant saying "yes" with sincere integrity and "no" with resolute compassion. It meant not shrinking to make others comfortable or tolerating behavior that chipped away at my worth.

When a man sees that you value yourself, including your emotions, your time, your body, he will do one of two things. He will either **rise to meet your standard** OR **walk away** because of his own inability or unwillingness to do so. Either outcome is protection.

Preparing your heart isn't just about being ready for love. It's about creating a foundation of wisdom, wholeness, and self-respect. When your heart is rooted in truth, you won't settle for counterfeit affection. You'll wait for the real thing with dignity and grace.

As you prepare your heart, it's also important to pray for your future spouse. Though you may not know who he is yet, your prayers have the power to cover him in protection, guidance, and spiritual growth. Proverbs 16:9 says, "In their hearts, humans plan their course, but the Lord establishes their steps." Even now, God can work in your future spouse's life, shaping him for your future together.

1. Praying for His Heart and His Walk with God

You want a husband who is grounded in his faith and is following God's will. It's important to start praying now that God strengthens his heart and character. Proverbs 4:23 reminds us to guard our hearts, and you should pray that your future spouse is doing the same.

PRAY:

"Lord, I pray for my future husband's heart. May You protect him and fill him with a deep love for You. Help him to be a man of integrity, strength, and godliness, someone who follows Your will above all else."

2. Praying for His Purpose

Just as God is shaping you, He is shaping your future spouse as well. Pray that he is growing in his calling, walking in God's purpose for his life, and becoming the man God has called him to be.

PRAY:

"Father, I pray that You guide my future husband in his journey. Lead him in Your purpose, protect him from distractions, and help him grow spiritually so that when we meet, we are both ready for the future You have planned for us."

REFLECT

Are you treating your own heart with the same care, honesty, and dignity that you desire from someone else? What boundaries or standards do you need to reinforce to protect your heart and prepare it for a love rooted in truth and respect?

_____

_____

_____

_____

_____

_____

_____

_____

_____

_____

_____

_____

_____

_____

_____

REFLECT

In what areas of your life (spiritual, emotional, relational) do you feel least prepared for marriage? What steps can you take to grow in these areas, even if marriage feels far off?

_____

_____

_____

_____

_____

_____

_____

_____

_____

_____

_____

_____

_____

_____

_____

_____

REFLECT

What kind of wife do you believe God is shaping you to be? How do your current habits, behaviors, and thoughts align with the biblical vision of a godly wife?

_____

_____

_____

_____

_____

_____

_____

_____

_____

_____

_____

_____

_____

_____

Embracing Singleness with Joy

Singleness is not a sentence; it's a sacred season. A time not of waiting to be chosen, but of being fully available to God. Paul reminds us that the unmarried woman has a unique opportunity: to be wholly devoted to the Lord without distraction. He said, "An unmarried woman or virgin is concerned about the Lord's affairs: Her aim is to be devoted to the Lord in both body and spirit." (1 Corinthians 7:34, NIV)

For many women, singleness can feel like a wilderness, but it can be a workshop, a time to examine your heart, your habits, and your healing. Before I could be ready for love, I had to take a hard look at myself. I had to deal with my own shortcomings. There were things in me, like impatience, emotional hurt, pride, even how I viewed men, that needed healing. If I entered a relationship without addressing those wounds, I would've brought unnecessary baggage with me. I spent my time getting closer to God, surrendering my will, and healing from some of the self-inflicted wounds from my past.

This season isn't about becoming perfect, though. It's about becoming whole. Ask yourself:

- Am I carrying unresolved pain from past relationships?
- Have I surrendered my insecurities and fears to God?
- Do I see singleness as lack—or as preparation?

When you work on yourself, you don't just prepare for a relationship—you protect your future from the damage of unhealed wounds. You build emotional strength, sharpen spiritual wisdom, and allow God to refine you.

Psalm 16:11 *"You make known to me the path of life; in your presence there is fullness of joy."* (ESV)

True joy isn't found in someone's arms; it's found in God's presence. As you deepen your walk with Him, you discover that solitude doesn't mean loneliness. It means space to grow: to travel, learn, serve, build, and dream.

While a healthy relationship does offer happiness. Contentment doesn't only come from partnership. It comes from purpose. It comes from waking up each day knowing who you are, whose you are, and where your peace comes from.

REFLECT

Ask yourself: Am I using this season of singleness to grow closer to God and heal emotionally or am I rushing past it in search of companionship?
What areas of my heart or character still need attention before you can build a healthy relationship with someone else?

_____

_____

_____

_____

_____

_____

_____

_____

_____

_____

_____

_____

_____

_____

REFLECT

How does your current relationship with God reflect the kind of woman you want to be in the future? Are you prioritizing His voice above all others, or are you distracted by external pressures?

_____

_____

_____

_____

_____

_____

_____

_____

_____

_____

_____

_____

_____

_____

_____

_____

Bearing Fruit

God isn't just preparing you to receive love, He's forming you into someone who can live love well. This happens through the cultivation of the **Fruit of the Spirit**. While the world may tell you to be bold, loud, and always "on guard," the Spirit invites you into something deeper, something holy.

Galatians 5:22–23 *"But the fruit of the Spirit is love, joy, peace, patience, kindness, goodness, faithfulness, gentleness and self-control. Against such things there is no law."* (NIV)

In a culture that encourages urgency and self-promotion, God calls us to grow in the Spirit, or to bear fruit that reflects His heart. Singleness isn't just about waiting for the right relationship, it's about becoming the right woman: one rooted in character, faith, and emotional strength witnessed in bearing fruit.

Let's take a look at **six key fruits** that prepare your heart for godly relationships:

🌿 Patience: Learning to Wait Without Withering

Patience is not just about waiting, it's about trusting. It's about believing that God's timing is wiser than your own and refusing to settle just because you're tired of being alone. It's knowing that God's delays are not denials and believing He's preparing something better than what you're tempted to settle for.

"The Lord is good to those who wait for him, to the soul who seeks him."
— Lamentations 3:25

🌱 Humility: Making Room for Grace

Humility releases the need to prove or perform. It allows you to see others and yourself through the eyes of grace. It's the soil in which healthy relationships grow. It keeps your heart teachable and reachable. It invites God to shape you and allows you to release the need to control or compete.

"He guides the humble in what is right and teaches them his way." — Psalm 25:9

🌸 Kindness: Living Love in Action

Kindness softens your responses and opens your heart. It isn't weakness, it's strength under control. True kindness says, "I will treat you with the dignity I desire for myself."

"Be kind and compassionate to one another…" — Ephesians 4:32

🌿 Gentleness: Strength with Sensitivity

Gentleness is often overlooked, but it's a vital sign of maturity. It tempers your tone, guards your reactions, and expresses love with care. In relationships, gentleness protects peace and fosters emotional safety.

"Let your gentleness be evident to all." — Philippians 4:5

🔒 Self-Control: Honoring God with Your Choices

Self-control is the quiet power that keeps you aligned with your values, even when your emotions or desires try to lead you astray. It's what helps you set boundaries, say no to temptation, and stay rooted in truth.

"Like a city whose walls are broken through is a person who lacks self-control." — Proverbs 25:28

⭐ Faithfulness: More Than a Feeling, a Covenant

Faithfulness isn't based on how you feel, it's rooted in what you've committed to. In a world that tells us to follow our hearts and change our minds when things get hard, God calls us to something deeper: covenant. Covenant is not a contract but rather a sacred promise, a spiritual agreement that stands even when feelings fade or circumstances shift.

"Know therefore that the Lord your God is God; he is the faithful God, keeping his covenant of love to a thousand generations…" — Deuteronomy 7:9 (NIV)

When you choose to be faithful in your relationship with God, especially during your season of singleness, you are saying, "I will keep showing up. I will trust You even when I don't understand. I will honor You, even when it costs me something." That's faithfulness. This kind of faithfulness forms the foundation that godly marriages are built on—steady, dependable, and spiritually grounded.

REFLECT

How are you cultivating the fruits of the Spirit in your life while waiting for your spouse? Reflect on how the fruits of the Spirit are manifesting in your daily life. What specific fruits do you need to nurture more intentionally while waiting for God's best?

_____

_____

_____

_____

_____

_____

_____

_____

_____

_____

_____

_____

_____

REFLECT

Which fruit of the Spirit is most evident in my life right now? How can you *better* cultivate the fruits of the Spirit in your life now, so that you are fully prepared to love and support your future husband in a Christlike way?

_____

_____

_____

_____

_____

_____

_____

_____

_____

_____

_____

_____

_____

_____

_____

REFLECT

How can cultivating gentleness and self-control protect my heart and shape healthier relationships in the future? What does faithfulness look like in my daily walk as a single woman spiritually, emotionally and relationally?

_____

_____

_____

_____

_____

_____

_____

_____

_____

_____

_____

_____

_____

_____

_____

_____

Honoring God with Your Body

One of the most sacred and often most challenging areas of obedience while waiting on your King is sexual restraint. The Bible calls it "fornication"—sexual intimacy outside the covenant of marriage—and God calls us to flee from it, not because He wants to withhold pleasure, but because He knows how deeply it affects our hearts, minds, and spirits.

I didn't always honor God in this area. There were times I entered relationships and compromised physically, believing that intimacy would lead to love. But it didn't. Instead, it left me with a shattered sense of self-worth and a strained connection with God. I gave so much of myself, including my body, only to realize I wasn't receiving the commitment I longed for.

I even had my son, my only child, thinking it would bring me closer to my longtime boyfriend at the time. I imagined that we would finally become a family. Instead of bringing us together, it revealed just how emotionally distant and unaligned we truly were. That choice, made out of hope and longing, only deepened my disappointment.

It wasn't until I surrendered this part of my life and chose celibacy that things truly began to shift. By the time I met my husband, Delroy, I had fully submitted my body and my boundaries to God. That decision, though difficult, brought me clarity, confidence, and peace. I was no longer trying to earn love through my body. I had already found love in God, and I walked into that new relationship already whole.

1 Cor. 6:19–20 *"Do you not know that your bodies are temples of the Holy Spirit, who is in you, whom you have received from God? You are not your own; you were bought at a price. Therefore honor God with your bodies."*

Your body is sacred. It's not a bargaining chip, a test of loyalty, or a pathway to commitment. It is the temple of the Holy Spirit (1 Corinthians 6:19–20), and when you honor God with your body, you invite His favor, protection, and presence into your journey. Sexual purity isn't just about waiting—it's about worth. It's a declaration that you trust God to fulfill your desire in His time, and that you believe you're worth being pursued, respected, and loved the way He designed.

REFLECT

In what ways have you sought love, validation, or connection through physical intimacy rather than through God's presence and affirmation? What has that cost you emotionally or spiritually?

_____

_____

_____

_____

_____

_____

_____

_____

_____

_____

_____

_____

_____

_____

REFLECT

What boundaries do you need to establish or strengthen to honor God with your body during this season of waiting? How can you invite Him into that commitment daily?

_____

_____

_____

_____

_____

_____

_____

_____

_____

_____

_____

_____

_____

_____

Work Out Your Faith

Becoming Her One Day at a Time

Step 1: **Create Sacred Space in Solitude**

"In quietness and trust is your strength." – Isaiah 30:15

Set aside 10–15 minutes each day this week to be alone with God—no phone, no distractions.

✏️ In your journal, write down one thing you're grateful for in your current season of solitude.

🙏 End your time with this prayer: *"Lord, help me find joy in Your presence and strength in my stillness."*

Step 2: **Embrace the Gift of Singleness**

"Her aim is to be devoted to the Lord in both body and spirit." – 1 Corinthians 7:34 (NIV)

💌 Write a letter to God describing what singleness feels like for you right now. Be honest. Then, write a second letter, this time, from your future self, encouraging you to enjoy this season and grow through it.

Step 3: **Practice the Fruit of the Spirit**

"But the fruit of the Spirit is love, joy, peace, patience, kindness, goodness, faithfulness, gentleness, and self-control." – Galatians 5:22–23

🕊️ Choose one fruit of the Spirit to focus on each day for the next **9 days**.

Each morning, ask: *"How can I express [patience, kindness, etc.] today?"*

Each evening, journal your experience: *Did I live this out? Where did I struggle? Where did I grow?*

AFFIRMATION
of
Faith

I am becoming the woman God has called me to be: whole, joyful, and content in every season. In solitude, I find strength and peace in His presence. I embrace this time of singleness as sacred, devoted fully to the Lord. Patience, humility, and kindness are bearing fruit in me through the Holy Spirit. I trust that God is shaping me with purpose, preparing me not just for someone else, but for my calling, my growth, and His glory.

Now, Write Your Own...

_____

_____

_____

_____

_____

_____

FOSTERING A PURPOSEFUL LIFE

As a single Christian woman, the waiting season is not a period of inactivity or loneliness. Instead, it is a unique and sacred time where God calls you to grow, serve, and thrive in your divine purpose. This isn't just about preparing for a future spouse; it's about preparing to be the woman God has called you to be in every aspect of your life. By embracing this time, you can walk in the fullness of who you are in Christ, finding joy and fulfillment in His presence, while deepening your faith and embracing your purpose.

Living Out Your Purpose

One of the most important things you can do while waiting is to pursue the calling God has placed on your life. This is your time to explore the gifts and talents He has given you and to use them to serve others, grow in your faith, and live out the unique purpose He has designed for you. Whether it's in your career, your ministry, or your personal passions, your purpose is not on hold while you wait for a future spouse. It is unfolding right now.

The Bible is filled with examples of individuals who lived out their calling, regardless of their relationship status. You can take inspiration from these stories and recognize that God has a plan for you that doesn't start when you get married. It starts now — as you are, where you are, and with what you already have.

Deborah was a prophetess and the only female judge in Israel. She wasn't just a wise counselor, though, she was also a military leader and spiritual guide. At a time when Israel was oppressed and afraid, God raised Deborah to lead with courage and divine wisdom. She didn't hesitate when Barak, the military commander, refused to go into battle without her. She boldly declared that the Lord would deliver the enemy into a woman's hands, and He did. Judges 5:7 states: "Villagers in Israel would not fight; they held back until I, Deborah, arose, until I arose, a mother in Israel."

She shows us that purpose doesn't always look traditional. Sometimes it means standing firm in strength, leadership, and faith, even when others hesitate.

One of the most dangerous lies we can believe as women is that fulfillment mainly comes from romantic relationships or marriage. As believers, we know that true fulfillment comes from Christ alone. We are complete in Him (Colossians 2:10), and no person or relationship can satisfy us the way that Jesus can. Look at Anna, the prophetess in Luke 2:36-38. Anna was an aged widow who had been married for only seven years before her husband died, but instead of wallowing in sorrow or seeking fulfillment in another relationship, she devoted her entire life to God. She spent her days in the temple, worshiping, fasting, and praying. Anna found her fulfillment in the presence of God, and because of her devotion, she was among the first few to acknowledge and honor baby Jesus. She confirmed the good news of the Messiah's arrival when Mary and Joseph brought him to the temple.

Anna's story teaches us that fulfillment comes not from earthly relationships, but from an intimate relationship with God. Her declaration of the Redeemer's presence fulfilled the prophecies and her purpose.

Psalm 16:11 *"You make known to me the path of life; in your presence, there is fullness of joy; at your right hand are pleasures forevermore."*

Mary Magdalene was once bound by seven demons, but Jesus delivered her completely. From that moment on, she became a devoted follower, traveling with Jesus and supporting His ministry. What's extraordinary is that Mary Magdalene was the first person Jesus appeared to after His resurrection, and He chose her to carry the message to the disciples.

In a time when women's voices were not culturally valued, God trusted Mary with the most important news in human history. Her past didn't disqualify her. In fact, it prepared her to walk closely with Jesus and speak boldly on His behalf. Jesus told her, "Go to my brothers and tell them..." (John 20:17, NIV)

Whether leading a nation like Deborah or being the first witness of the risen Savior like Mary Magdalene, God uses women with willing hearts, no matter their past or position. Your purpose is not limited by your circumstances but empowered by your obedience.

REFLECT

If you knew that God was shaping you for something far greater than just marriage, how would that change how you prepare yourself now? What steps can you take to walk in alignment with God's purpose for you in this season?

_____

_____

_____

_____

_____

_____

_____

_____

_____

_____

_____

_____

_____

_____

REFLECT

Do you believe that your value or purpose will be enhanced by marriage? Examine if you're placing too much emphasis on marriage as a measure of success. How can you rediscover your value as it stands in Christ alone, apart from any relationship?

Understanding the Path to Your Purpose

For a long time, I had a void that I just couldn't seem to fill, and deep down, I knew it was because I wasn't walking in God's purpose for my life. My journey toward fulfillment began with an honest look in the mirror. I had to silence the lie that I had missed my chance. I had to tell myself: "You're not too old. You still have time. God's not finished with you yet.'"

That season of self-reflection revealed a painful but powerful truth: the emptiness I was feeling wasn't about singleness, age, or even external success. It was a spiritual void, a result of not living out the purpose God had planted within me. I was running from God because I knew that coming to Him would require me to subdue my flesh. When I finally surrendered my will and ways, I expected some kind of prophetic declaration about my purpose, but it never occurred. Over time, I came to understand that purpose isn't always loud or obvious. Sometimes it's a gentle tug in your spirit—a longing to do more, love deeper, and serve wider. When you ignore that tug, you feel the effects: restlessness, dissatisfaction, and even regret.

God can and does use both our past and present to align us with His purpose. Nothing is wasted, and I am a living witness. I finally got married at age 55, after making more dating and relationship mistakes than I care to admit. In fact, I made so many that I could write a book, and that's exactly what I've done. I've created three journals, so far, for people who are single, dating, or even married. Looking back, I realize I was on my purpose path the entire time. God knew I would struggle with obedience for far too long, but He still used that for His glory and for the edification of those who will read and learn from my journey. My hope is that others won't have to go through what I did.

I believe that our purpose is to fulfill God's will in whatever we do. And if it doesn't align with His will, it won't make sense because something will suffer. Most often, that something is you. Of course, your future spouse will need to be part of the journey, someone who supports, honors, and even complements your purpose or calling. However, while you're waiting, that's not your responsibility to figure out. You don't have to go searching for someone to complete your purpose. God is perfectly capable of aligning your path with the right person at the right time. Your job right now is to trust and obey, to follow His leading, cultivate your gifts, and walk in your assignment today. God didn't ask you to find someone. He asked you to follow Him. And in doing so, you'll find everything you need, including the right partner for the journey ahead.

REFLECT

What does "purpose" mean to you personally, and how do you believe God is calling you to live with purpose while you wait?

_____

_____

_____

_____

_____

_____

_____

_____

_____

_____

_____

_____

_____

_____

_____

REFLECT

Are you resisting God's purpose for your life because it challenges your comfort, control, or familiar habits? How has God already been using your past, both your mistakes and your milestones, to prepare you for the purpose He's calling you to?

_____

_____

_____

_____

_____

_____

_____

_____

_____

_____

_____

_____

_____

Establishing Godly Friendships and Community

As a single Christian woman, it's essential to surround yourself with godly friends who will encourage you, hold you accountable, and walk with you through this season. Proverbs 27:17 reminds us, **"As iron sharpens iron, so one person sharpens another."** Godly friendships are a source of strength, and they help you grow spiritually and emotionally. Being single doesn't mean being isolated or lonely. It's a time to build a strong community that will sharpen and support you in your walk with Christ. You will want to be around people who know how to pray and encourages you in your purpose.

Ecclesiastes 4:9-10 *"Two are better than one, because they have a good return for their labor: If either of them falls down, one can help the other up."*

The friendship between Mary and Elizabeth is one of the most beautiful examples of godly companionship in the Bible (Luke 1:39–45). These two women were at very different stages of life. Elizabeth, older and once barren, now miraculously pregnant with John the Baptist; Mary, a young virgin carrying the Son of God. Both were living through unbelievable, divine assignments, and yet they found strength and safety in each other's presence. When Elizabeth heard Mary's greeting, her baby leaped in her womb, and she was filled with the Holy Spirit, exclaiming, "Blessed are you among women, and blessed is the child you will bear!"

Mary stayed with Elizabeth for three months, long enough to be nurtured, strengthened, and affirmed in what God was doing in her life. Their friendship was not based on convenience or popularity. It was **rooted in purpose** and powered by faith. Elizabeth didn't compete with Mary. She celebrated her. She didn't question her story. She confirmed it through the Holy Spirit.

You don't need friends who only validate your feelings. You need friends who strengthen your faith. Women who see the hand of God on your life and call it out when you forget. Women who will remind you, "You are blessed and highly favored," even when you feel overwhelmed or overlooked. Godly friendships aren't just helpful, they're holy connections that prepare and support you as you walk out your purpose.

What Godly Friendship Looks Like:

- *Spirit-filled affirmation* – Friends who speak life into what God is birthing in you
- *Safe spaces to grow* – Environments where you don't have to explain your obedience or defend your calling
- *Mutual encouragement* – A two-way flow of joy, prayer, and support through life's transitions
- *Celebratory recognition, no jealousy* – Rejoicing over each other's breakthroughs as if they were your own

One of the biggest challenges my husband and I faced early in our marriage was the company I kept. I had too many friends, many of whom were not walking in alignment with godly values. Some of them were living recklessly, and because I was constantly around them, I found myself in environments that didn't reflect the woman I claimed to be. We were going to bars, casinos, and places that did not honor God or support the life I said I wanted.

Delroy called me out on it. He said, "How can you say you're a Christian when you're surrounding yourself with women who live in direct opposition to that? How is it that they're all the same, but you say you're different?" He wasn't wrong. One of the women closest to me at the time was even involved with a married man, and I was tolerating that as normal. It was a wake-up call.

If I wanted a marriage built on mutual respect and spiritual integrity, I had to make a change. I had to "clean house," as they say, letting go of several friendships that were not helping me grow but pulling me backward. It was hard, but it was necessary. In that process, I learned that who you surround yourself with has a direct impact on your peace, purpose, and spiritual covering.

Even if we have strong intentions or spiritual convictions, the people we consistently surround ourselves with influence our mindset, behaviors, and spiritual health. Over time, unwise associations can wear down our standards, blur our values, and subtly lead us away from the path God has called us to walk. A key scripture that directly supports the idea that bad company can corrupt even the best intentions is: "Do not be misled: 'Bad company corrupts good character'" (1 Cor. 15:33 NIV). Thus, relationships are not neutral. They either pull you closer to God or farther away.

REFLECT

Do the people you spend the most time with draw you closer to God or distract you from who He's calling you to become? Who in your life affirms your God-given purpose and encourages your spiritual growth?

_____

_____

_____

_____

_____

_____

_____

_____

_____

_____

_____

_____

_____

_____

REFLECT

Are there any friendships you need to release or invest in more intentionally in order to walk in purpose with clarity and peace? How can you go about this?

_____

_____

_____

_____

_____

_____

_____

_____

_____

_____

_____

_____

_____

_____

Being a Good Steward of Time & Gifts

One of the greatest temptations during a season of waiting is to become idle, thinking that nothing important is happening relationally until your future spouse arrives. But God has entrusted you with time, talents, and spiritual gifts that He wants you to use and develop now. The Bible teaches us that each of us will be held accountable for how we manage what God has given us. Waiting is not a time to pause or waste. It's a time to grow, serve, and invest in what matters most for eternity.

Being a good steward of your time means recognizing the value of every moment and asking God how you can live wisely and purposefully. It's about waking up each day with the intention of making it count for the Kingdom. Likewise, stewarding your gifts means understanding that you are uniquely equipped for specific good works, which God prepared in advance for you to do (Ephesians 2:10). This season is your opportunity to cultivate those gifts and use them for His glory, regardless of whether you're married or single.

In Ephesians 5:15-16, Paul urges us to "be very careful, how you live—not as unwise but as wise, making the most of every opportunity, because the days are evil." We live in a world filled with distractions, temptations, and pressures to conform to unhealthy patterns. Stewarding your time means resisting those distractions and living intentionally. This season is a perfect opportunity to invest in your spiritual growth, develop your relationship with God, and pursue the things that matter most to you—whether that's a ministry, career goals, serving others, or personal development.

Psalm 90:12: *"Teach us to number our days, that we may gain a heart of wisdom."*

Your time is valuable, and what you do with it now will shape your future. Stewarding your gifts involves:

- **Developing your skills**: Whether through education, practice, or seeking mentorship, take this time to sharpen your abilities so you are fully equipped for the opportunities God will bring.
- **Serving others**: Your gifts are meant to bless others. Ask God how you can serve your church, community, or those around you with the talents He has given you.

- **Using your gifts for the Kingdom**: Don't wait for a future spouse to step into your calling. The purpose God has for you is for the here and now. Seek opportunities to use your gifts in meaningful ways.

Romans 12:6-8: *"We have different gifts, according to the grace given to each of us. If your gift is prophesying, then prophesy in accordance with your faith; if it is serving, then serve; if it is teaching, then teach..."*

The Parable of the Talents in Matthew 25:14-30 is a powerful illustration of stewardship. In the story, a master entrusts his servants with different amounts of money (talents) while he is away. Two of the servants invest and multiply what they have been given, but one servant, out of fear and complacency, hides his talent and does nothing with it. The master rewards the faithful servants but rebukes the one who wasted his opportunity. This parable speaks directly to how we should handle the gifts, talents, and resources

God has entrusted to us. Sitting idle or waiting for "the perfect time" to use them will only result in missed opportunities.

God has gifted you with unique talents, and this season is your chance to multiply what He has given you. You may not know when your future spouse will come, but your purpose remains the same—use your gifts now and trust that God will bless your efforts.

It's tempting to view waiting as a passive experience, but God is calling you to be active in your growth, purpose, and service. By becoming a good steward of your time and gifts, you are not only preparing yourself for your future spouse, but more importantly, you are preparing yourself to fulfill the unique calling God has placed on your life. Your purpose is not delayed because you are single. It's happening right now in this season, as your purpose is a path, not a destination.

Waiting isn't wasting time. It's the time to:
- **Deepen your relationship with God**: Use this time to cultivate intimacy with Him, through prayer, worship, and Bible study.
- **Pursue personal growth**: Take this time to grow emotionally, mentally, and spiritually, becoming the best version of yourself.
- **Invest in your future**: Whether through developing your career, ministry, or personal skills, this is a season of investment.

REFLECT

If you were to meet your future spouse tomorrow, would they find you actively living out your purpose or waiting idly? What would they learn about your relationship with God based on how you are using this time?

_____

_____

_____

_____

_____

_____

_____

_____

_____

_____

_____

_____

_____

_____

_____

_____

REFLECT

Have you truly embraced the idea that singleness is a gift from God or do you view it as a season of lack? How has your perception of singleness influenced your ability to live with purpose? Are you embracing it as a time of growth or resenting it as an obstacle? What would change if you saw it as a blessing?

_____

_____

_____

_____

_____

_____

_____

_____

_____

_____

_____

_____

_____

Work Out Your Faith

Living with Purpose on Purpose

Step 1: **Meditate on God's Promise**
"'For I know the plans I have for you,' declares the Lord, 'plans to prosper you and not to harm you, plans to give you hope and a future.'" – Jeremiah 29:11

📖 Read this verse aloud.
✏️ Write a short response in your journal: What does this verse say to me personally about my life right now?

Step 2: See Purpose in Preparation
Nothing is wasted—your past, your pain, your waiting. It's all preparing you.

📆 Reflect on a past experience that challenged you but helped shape you.
🖍️ Write a few sentences about how that moment prepared you for something greater. What did you learn? How did you grow?

Step 3: Discover Your Strengths and Weaknesses
Strengths and weaknesses, God uses both for His glory.

🍀 On a sheet of paper, create two columns:
   Column 1: "My Strengths"
   Column 2: "Areas I'm Growing In or Need Growth"
✏️ List at least 3 items under each.
Ask God to show you how He wants to use both in your journey of purpose.

Work Out Your Faith

Living with Purpose on Purpose

Step 4: **Activate Your Spiritual Gifts**
"We have different gifts, according to the grace given to each of us..."
– Romans 12:6

✝ Reflect on what comes naturally to you—encouraging others, serving, teaching, creating, organizing?

✏ Write down 1–2 gifts you believe God has given you.

💬 Then write one way you can use one of those gifts this week—no matter how small.

Remember: Purpose is not a destination. It's a way of living. Each step, each prayer, and each gift you embrace brings you closer to becoming the woman God designed you to be.

AFFIRMATION
of
Faith

God has a plan for my life, one filled with hope, purpose, and a future. Every season, even the waiting ones, is preparing me for something greater. I embrace both my strengths and my weaknesses, knowing that His grace is made perfect in my imperfections. I celebrate the unique gifts He has placed within me, and I choose to walk boldly in the calling He has entrusted to me. My life has meaning, and I am living it on purpose, for His glory.

Now, Write Your Own...

_____

_____

_____

_____

_____

_____

CONCLUSION: BECOMING WHOLE & READY FOR LOVE

As you come to the end of this guide and journal, remember that this journey of waiting is not passive. Instead, it's an active process of growth, faith, and preparation. Every step you take now is shaping the woman God is calling you to be. You've explored your identity in Christ, the dangers of settling, the importance of trusting God's timing, and how to build a purposeful life while waiting. You've also learned that waiting is not just about finding a future spouse but about becoming the person God has designed you to be.

"Waiting on your King from the King" is not about sitting idle or yearning for what's to come. It's about living fully in the present with intention, stewarding your gifts, and allowing God to shape your heart. You are already enough in Christ, and your worth is found in Him alone, not in a future relationship or any external circumstance.

Again, this season is not about passivity; it's about becoming a better you. Becoming the best version of yourself is not about perfection, but about alignment with who God created you to be. It's about healing, growing, trusting, and learning to love yourself through God's eyes. The love you seek in a mate should be a reflection of the love you've already cultivated within. You attract what you are ready to sustain. So become the kind of woman who embodies the same faith, integrity, patience, joy, and wholeness you desire in a partner. Let your waiting be purposeful, your healing be intentional, and your identity be rooted in Christ because the woman you are becoming is worthy of the love you are waiting for.

Trust that God's plan for you is far greater than you could ever imagine. When you align yourself with His timing, His Word, and His purpose, the right person will enter your life at the right time. But more importantly, you will have grown into the woman of faith, strength, and purpose that He's called you to be.

REFLECT

What qualities have I developed during this season that reflect the kind of love, patience, and faith I hope to experience in a future relationship?

_____

_____

_____

_____

_____

_____

_____

_____

_____

_____

_____

_____

_____

_____

REFLECT

If the man I'm praying for met me today, would he see in me the same character, wholeness, and spiritual maturity that I hope to see in him? If not, what area is God still inviting me to grow in?

_____

_____

_____

_____

_____

_____

_____

_____

_____

_____

_____

_____

_____

FINAL PRAYER

Dear Heavenly Father,

I surrender my desires, my timeline, and my future into Your hands. I trust that Your plans are good, and I pray for continued strength as I walk in faith and patience. Help me to grow in wisdom, love, and purpose, becoming the woman You've designed me to be. Guide my steps, Lord, and prepare my heart for whatever is ahead, knowing that You are my ultimate source of joy and fulfillment.

Thank You for walking with me through this season of waiting and refinement. I surrender every fear and fixation to You. Help me to trust Your plan more than my own, and to find joy in becoming the woman You've called me to be. Teach me to love myself and others as You love me, and to rest in the truth that I am already complete in Christ. Teach me how to love You through obedience to your will, ways and Word with a servant's heart. As I wait, prepare my heart, protect my peace, and position me for a love that reflects Your glory.

In Jesus' name, Amen.

Keep moving forward in faith, embracing the beauty of this season, and trusting the God who knows your future and holds your heart.

www.ingramcontent.com/pod-product-compliance
Lightning Source LLC
Chambersburg PA
CBHW040856120626
46551CB00001B/40